Glory to God in the highest.

I0620422

DANCE *as*
DAVID DANCED
The Return of Davidic Worship

RHODA BANKS

Dance as David Danced
Copyright © 2015 by Rhoda Banks. All rights reserved.

No part of this publication may be reproduced, stored in a retrieval system or transmitted in any way by any means, electronic, mechanical, photocopy, recording or otherwise without the prior permission of the author except as provided by USA copyright law.

Unless otherwise stated, Scripture quotations are taken from the New Spirit Filled Life Bible, New King James Version by Jack Hayford. 2002. Used by permission. All rights reserved.

Cover design by Rtor Maghuyop
Interior design by Caypeeline Casas

Published in the United States of America

ISBN: 979-8-218-32293-9
1. Religion / Christian Rituals & Practice / Worship & Liturgy
2. Religion / Messianic Judaism
14.12.13

Acknowledgments

I would like to acknowledge the Lord Jesus for leading me to write this book on Davidic worship and for giving me divine revelation concerning Amos 9:11–12. Lord you are awesome, and I thank you from the bottom of my heart for instructing me and giving me the resources to complete this project.

Also I would like to thank Sid Roth and his ministry. Gold nuggets of revelation were gleaned from Sid and the guests that he had on his show, Shane Warren and Keith Duncan, both Worship leaders. David Herzog's prophetic insights and revelation concerning Israel brought life to this book also.

I would also like to thank Chris Zimmerman Machado, and Pastor/Worship Leader, Mike Smith for all the encouragement and help they offered me on this subject matter.

I also want to extend thanks to Damon Stuart, Worship Leader and Recording Artist for endorsing this book. Although we have never met personally, he has a heart of worship for the Lord, which is reflected in his willingness to endorse this book.

Reverend Kathy Lombardo—also a special thank you for all the support and help with this project and direction concerning end time events.

Also I would like to extend thanks to David Farrell. Thanks for your dedication to minister the gospel and be a blessing to Recovery Ministries.

A special thank you also goes out to Peg Avery, for her help and guidance in bringing this book to life, and going the extra mile.

ENDORSEMENTS

"If you want to transform your life and elevate your worship to a place where you will meet with the Lord, this is the book to read. Be prepared to be changed when you enter into Davidic Worship."

Rev. Kathy Lombardo
Registrar, Administrator and Teacher
GEM Bible Institute

"The river of God's love and supernatural power flowing through our lives, homes, and churches is something that every end-time friend of God desires. The key to accessing and drinking from this river is unglued worship. Rhoda Banks's *The Return of Davidic Worship*, is a valuable tool in exploring David's tabernacle, and its model of intimacy and passion."

Michael Smith, Lead Pastor
Ignite Church

"Rhoda taps into the heart of God with Davidic Worship. A Rhema Word for those who desire to worship the Lord in spirit and truth…".

Day Gospel Rap Artist, Davidic Records
www.day the untouchable.com

"I have read many books on worship that were instructional, practical and even anointed but I would have to say, that *Dance as David Danced, The Return of Davidic Worship* by Rhoda Banks is one of my top three favorites. While the book is practical and educational regarding the study of worship; Rhoda brings a fresh perspective about true worship as though she was writing from the heart of the Father.

This book should be a prerequisite for all worship leaders/Pastors who desire the presence of the Lord in every service but even more than that, this book should be read by anyone who longs to worship the King of Kings in spirit and truth. If you desire to cultivate an atmosphere of worship in your life and or ministry and you've asked God to give you a heart like David's concerning worship, then this book is definitely for you!"

Damon Stuart
Damon Stuart Worship Ministries
www.damonstuart.com

"This book should be part of every worship leaders arsenal. The truths that Rhoda Banks has uncovered are timeless and relevant for all who seek to worship the Father in spirit and truth. The amazing thing about the truth you will find in this book it that it spreads beyond the walls of religion and any one denomination. I wish I had a resource like this when I first started out in leading worship however it also touches on our personal worship to the Father too. I am certain that you too will appreciate the richness of this book."

Pastor Tim Fuest
Lead Pastor, Worship Leader, Song Writer
Hope in Life Church

TABLE OF CONTENTS

PART 1

PART II

PART 1

INTRODUCTION

Dance as David Danced,
The Return of Davidic Worship

I wrote this book as a way to glorify the Lord. Worshipping "in spirit and truth" (John 4:24) brings God's anointing and power on the scene as we give God our best. He is pleased as we worship Him and express thanksgiving. Praising Him in the beauty of His holiness allows our spirit to become saturated with His presence which brings fullness of joy.

As we press through into the Glory Zone, we enter into the throne room where God meets with us. He wants us to have a personal relationship with Him, so we can partake of heavenly realities while living in an earthly body. By making a determination to press through all the voices and distractions, we find that we are able to hear God's voice. We must believe that He is interested in our lives and wants us to be blessed.

We need to pray the Scriptures and declare God's favor over our lives. To exercise faith, we speak to the mountain in our lives and believe that our dreams are coming true. As David ushered in a new way of worship, we also pray, praise, and proclaim to enter into a more intimate way of relating to the Lord, thus bringing His presence into our lives. God wants us to rely on Him in times of trouble and to trust Him. He wants us to keep our eyes on Him and be the focus of our lives.

As the times get more perilous, we will see an increase in those who need our care and counsel in their lives. By staying prayed up and keeping our relationship with the Lord up to date, we will be ready for all that will transpire. There will be a great outpouring of the Holy Spirit, which will bring many into the Kingdom. But we need to give God all the glory and to be steadfast in our faith when we see a lot of shaking going on.

The end time harvest is dependent on keeping ourselves stirred up and in love with Jesus. When we allow God to be our all-in-all, we are able to live in the strength and power of the Lord. As we walk in the new man, we are able to love the unlovable and bring God great glory. We are able to be fruitbearers when we allow God's word to take root in our hearts.

By singing a spontaneous song, we initiate the movement of heavenly beings who co-labor with us, in bringing in the harvest of souls. We are being commissioned to sing the promises of God and to release His will into the atmosphere to bring change and healing. The words we speak will set into motion angels that respond to our words of faith and work to see it accomplished. So, as we pray in the Spirit we release

God's will for our lives and allow our words to birth the promises of God.

The end time harvest is dependent on our relationship with Israel and as we reach out to her in her time of need, we set ourselves up for blessings. In the end times we will see an increase in hostility to Israel, and many will seek to devour her. But as we realize Israel's place in provoking revival of the nations, we will come to her aid and seek to be a blessing. The prosperity of our nation depends on our relationship with Israel and those who love her will prosper. It's time to renew our mind and to seek Him with our whole hearts so we can hear His voice and be used to usher in the great harvest of souls.

My hope is that in reading this book, you will enter into a more intimate relationship with the Lord, not limited to a Sunday morning experience. As you press into prayer mixed with praise you will usher in His presence, where your joy will be made full. Joy comes as a result of pressing past the distractions, into a place of praise, where He meets us and bids us to come into His chamber, where He lives. Praise allows us to come up higher in our devotion to the Lord. When our hearts are transformed, we are able to be molded into His image. Let's come into the place of high praise so we can become all that He has destined for us, even before the foundation of the world.

In Christ's love,
Rhoda Banks

Intimacy with God

Worship reaches the very heart of God. He is a rewarder of those who diligently seek Him (Hebrews 11:6). Psalms 22:3 states, "But you are holy, enthroned in the praises of Israel." The word *enthroned* means that God is exalted and placed on a throne by the praises of His people. *Enthrone* also means to marry. Jesus is our heavenly bridegroom, and as we exalt Him with our whole heart, He comes to partner with us. It's the high praises that enthrones Him, the passionate longing of a bride that is seeking for her bridegroom. He delights in our desire to be with Him and to capture His heart.

Song of Solomon 2:10-13 reveals the Shulamite woman's need to come away with her bridegroom, to be transparent and to trust again. The walls of our heart are melting, as we determine to give Him all that would come between us.

My beloved spoke and said to me;

> Rise up, my love, my fair one. And come away. For lo, the winter is past, The rain is over and gone, The flowers appear on the earth, The time of singing has

come, And the voice of the turtledove, Is heard in our land. The fig tree puts forth green figs, And the vines with the tender grapes Give a good smell. Rise up, my love, my fair one, And come away!

God is enthroned as we give Him first place in our lives. He wants a bride who is completely given over to Him so He can reign in our hearts without a rival. He wants a people so enthralled with Him that everything else palls in comparison. As we keep ourselves stirred up in His love, He is able to make Himself known to us and reveal His mysteries. When our hearts are on fire, we are able to see God high and lifted up on His throne. The praises of a sincere believer is a sweet savor in His nostrils. He enjoys our intimate fellowship and comes to reside (live) among and in us. Our sweet communion with the Lord brings Him on the scene. His presence is what we are after. The atmosphere created during worship is a composite of the spiritual condition of the worshipper's heart and spirit. As we allow His spirit to saturate our hearts, we become taken up in His glory. No substitutes will do.

When we capture His heart with our heartfelt confession of sin, He is able to bring us into the very throne room of His presence. We enter in by the shed blood of the Lamb. Nothing else will suffice. We sprinkle His blood as we move into the throne room, singing praises of thanksgiving. He desires that we come boldly and unashamed. Psalm 24:3–5 says,

"Who may ascend into the hill of the Lord?
Or who may stand in His holy place?
He who has clean hands and a pure heart.
Who has not lifted up his soul to an idol,
Nor sworn deceitfully.
He shall receive blessing from the Lord,
And righteousness from the God of his salvation."

Worship allows us to ascend His holy hill. We gain access to His presence, and as we do, we gain strategies to wage war as we descend.

ACTIVATING GOD'S PROMISE

We need revelation to war. As God reveals Himself to us, we are able to speak it into existence. He wants us to know His voice, so we can discern His will. His word is His will. God gave us a model on how to pray and what to pray to bring about a desired outcome. The Lord's Prayer is an example. Also as we pray in the Spirit, we are speaking God's perfect will into existence. It's not what we think is happening but rather what God says is going to take place.

We need to ask for a *rhema* word (inspired by the Lord) that will boost our faith level and cause us to believe beyond what we see happening in the natural. We are being commissioned to pray His word so we can take dominion over the lies that the enemy would try to throw our way. We know that as we pray God's perfect will into existence, no demon in hell can stop it. We are able to speak the very words of God to see turnaround in our lives. It's time to decree and declare that God is working to bring us into a place of restoration. The promises of God are entered into by faith, and as we bring our belief (our heart) in line with what we declare, we are able to see God's hand of activation in our midst.

One of my favorite resources on the importance of proclaiming God's word over your circumstance is Cindy Trimm's book *Commanding Your Morning*. She stresses how, as we speak God's word, He is able to perform it and bring it into existence. She talks about making decrees and has many declarations at the back of the book, which are very empowering.

God will bring to pass His promises in our lives as we seek Him wholeheartedly. He moves in response to our hunger and our willingness to speak His will into existence. A greater manifestation of the Lord's power and authority is available to believers. We need to ask Jesus to baptize us with the Holy Spirit, with the evidence of speaking in tongues. Then we are endowed with spiritual power from on high to be an effective witness. We need to pray for a hunger for the end-time harvest of souls. The workers are few, but when we enlist in God's army, we are equipped and made ready. Those who bring God great glory will be able to teach and preach even in the midst of great upheaval. They will teach God's priniciples empowered by His spirit, to bring in the harvest of souls. It's a time of upheaval, but as God's people avail themselves to speak to those who are in their sphere of influence, many people will be saved. It takes a persevering spirit to offset all that would seek to destroy our witness. A determination must be made to keep ourselves unstained from the world. Fear and intimidation should not stop us from sharing our witness. We have to remain convinced that God is working in our lives, to see His purposes come to pass. We are His handiwork, created to do good works even before the foundation of the world.

God will take care of, and provide for, those who worship Him "in spirit and truth" (John 4:24). They will see God's hand operating in their lives. The Lord desires that we walk in holiness, that we put His word first in our lives. The true worshipper worships Him in the beauty of His holiness, because as we revere His holiness, we worship Him in all His glory. The true worshippers seek Him and revere Him as Lord and Savior. It's doing the will of God from the heart. We need the Holy Spirit's divine enablement to give us God's perspective. By doing His will, we allow Him to move unhindered in our hearts. When we allow God's will to take hold in our lives, we become His mouthpieces and gain wisdom in the fiery furnace. As our hears are purified, then we are able to partake in His majesty and see Him as Lord in all situations. By preparing our hearts and removing the hindrances, we allow the Holy Spirit to groom us to move into a new level of anointing and power.

Praise elevates the bar of holiness and allows our spirit to reach heights that will bring us into the throne room so He can pour out His spirit in an abundant measure.

When we meet Him in our worship, God meets our needs and pushes the veil back so we can revel in His glory. The glory that was present in the Garden is but a foretaste of what we will see in heaven, but as we press through into the holy of holies, we enter into a place of unspeakable joy, as we are being transformed into His image. We need only to remain in this holy place so we can be filled and taken to a place of consuming love. His love compels us to stay and linger in His presence so we can be partakers of His majesty. We must linger and allow the Holy Spirit to stir our hearts to repentance, so we can experience Him in the glory of His holiness.

Our God is a consuming fire, and as we keep the fire burning on the altar of our hearts, we hear our good shepherd calling us to come to Him so He can fill us with the power of His all-consuming love. The love of the Father burns off the chaff that confines us and tries to entangle. As we allow this fire to burn off the chaff, we are able to contain and carry the splendor of His presence. By keeping ourselves filled with His presence, we become partakers of His divine nature and fire carriers who proclaim God's message to a lost and dying world.

We release His glory and power as we come up to the high place of worship and descend into war. We war in the spirit realm as we bring His glory to the earth realm because the glory demands that we stay on fire and in constant communication with the Lord. It's imperative that we hold up our shields to do warfare in the heavenly realm so we can enter into His promises. We need to keep His word ever before us so we can remain steadfast in our lives. The word is an anchor for our souls. God's word when spoken releases faith and miracles. It contains spiritual manna that enables us to grow and to do great exploits.

To do battle, we must remain armed and ready, as the enemy roams around looking for those he can devour. We gain authority to advance by praising God. No wonder the devil would try to stop it.

For we do not wrestle against flesh and blood, but against principalities, against powers, against the rulers of the darkness of this age, against spiritual hosts of wickedness in the heavenly places. "Therefore take up the whole armor of God, that you may be able to withstand in the evil day, and having done all, to stand" (Ephesians 6:12-13).

As a soldier prepares for battle, so we must listen to our Commanding Officer. God will execute judgment on our enemies and equip us, with a strategy as we take our position on the wall.

The battle needs to be enforced in the spiritual realm, before it can manifest in the natural. When we use our spiritual weapons, we are able to withstand the attacks of the enemy, and gain ground. It's time for the people of God to rise up, putting on the full armor of God daily.

Keeping Your Dreams Alive

Nehemiah was a man of vision. He was governor under King Artaxerxes. He saw that the walls and gates of Jerusalem were in disrepair. He asked and obtained permission from the king to repair it. But as his team worked, they received much opposition and scorn from others. They prayed to the Lord and, as a result, found out about a plan to stop their progress. So, Nehemiah set up armed men behind the walls where it was least protected. He also used other weapons to fight and appointed watchmen on the walls. Meanwhile, his enemies continued to taunt him to come off the wall and stop the building. He refused and continued the building until he reached completion.

At the dedication of the wall, Nehemiah appointed two large thanksgiving choirs to praise the Lord, and sacrifices were offered. Joy was proclaimed that day (Nehemiah 12:31,43). The completion of the wall provided security from enemy attacks and ensured that worship would continue without interference.

Praise is a restorative tonic that allows us to stand strong. We must stay on red alert by using this tonic liberally, knowing that what the Lord has started, He will finish. As we build for the Lord, we need to stay focused and not be distracted.

Many people have come off the wall discouraged, but we must encourage ourselves in the Lord. David knew how to do this by recounting the times the Lord showed himself faithful in coming through. Hebrews 10:32 encourages us to call to remembrance the former days in which, after you were illuminated, you endured a great struggle with sufferings.

Rick Renner in his book *Sparkling Gems: Sparkling Gems from the Greek, 365 Greek Word Studies for Every Day of the Year to Sharpen Your Understanding of God's Word* enlarges on this verse by saying, "Your divine calling, your God given dream, must be an illumination in your heart that you call to remembrance over and over again. Call to remembrance how God first spoke to you, and meditate on the promise He made to you. This will help you get past the weariness that's trying to pull you down. Keep your dream shining brilliantly in your heart and mind—a powerful illumination and revelation that lights your way through any darkness the enemy might bring against you![1]"

---

[1]   Rick Renner, *Sparkling Gems from the Greek*, Tulsa, Oklahoma, Teach All Nations, 2003.

Begin to praise Him from your innermost being. Allow Him to speak to you and declare that you are entering into a place of full restoration and that circumstances are turning around in Jesus's name. Do not forsake the work of your hands, for you will reap in due time if you don't give up. As you persevere, God will cause your barren places to be inhabited and overflow with blessings. The breaker (Jesus) will break through areas of resistance and will make the crooked places straight. Begin to decree and declare that you are being led and that the breaker is coming. He is able to accomplish everything He has promised because He is faithful to His word.

Keeping our eyes on the Lord and trusting Him is imperative in moving ahead. Though our faith being more precious than gold is being tested, we must continue to stand in the evil day and not lose hope. There will be a day of recompense for the faithful.

He will bring us into our destiny as we war for our inheritance. We war by decreeing and declaring that we are being taken into God's provision and that there will be no more delay in seeing the promise fulfilled.

I believe we are entering into a season where we will begin to see the fulfillment of destiny, but there must be a consecration to God's ways to enter into the fullness of what He has planned. No longer can we rely on feelings to guide us, but as we submit to God's will, we are made ready to enter into all that He has promised. "Delight your-

self also in the Lord; And He will give you the desires
of your heart" (Psalm 37:4). By giving over to the Lord
our desires, He is able to take our offering and give us
back more than what we expect in return. We are being
prepared to step into our destiny, so we can be all that
the Lord has ordained. His timing is perfect and His plans
for us will not disappoint. We are His instruments of glory
and grace on the earth today, as we allow His winnowing
fork to have its way.

As we keep God's word and allow the Holy Spirit to
reign in our lives, we are able to speak His words to a lost
and dying world.

We need the *ruah* (breath of God) to blow afresh on
us so we can refresh others with God's touch and care.
Every time we move under the anointing, we are expelling
a measure of the breath of God.

God is raising up an army of anointed, prophetic,
interceding, and worshipping warriors that will release the
very sounds of heaven and birth heaven's directives into
the earth realm. We represent Him as we go forth releasing His will into our sphere of influence. We must carry
God's presence in our midst so we can bring Him glory. He
wants us to stay connected to His Spirit during the day
so we can hear what the Spirit is saying. The Lord wants
us to share His message of good news to those who have
lost hope.

Songs Of Deliverance

When the heavens seem like brass, we need to let Praise and Worship lead the way. We are being prepared to enter into the Promised Land, but we must proclaim that the Lord is bringing us into a place of expansion. We need to proclaim this by singing praises and spiritual song in the midst of our Jericho.

Isaiah 54:1–5 states,

> Sing O barren,
> You who have not borne!
> Break forth into singing and cry aloud,
> You who have not labored with
> child!
> For more are the children of the desolate
> Than the children of the married woman.
> Enlarge the place of your tent
> And let them stretch out the curtains
> of your dwellings;
> Do not spare;
> Lengthen your cords.
> And strengthen your stakes.

For you shall expand to the right and to the left,
And your descendants will inherit the nations,
And make the desolate cities inhabited.
Do not fear, for you will not be
ashamed,
Neither be disgraced, for you will not
be put to shame;
For you will forget the shame of your youth,
And not remember the reproach
of your widowhood anymore.
For your Maker is your husband,
The Lord of hosts is His name,
And your redeemer is the Holy One
of Israel,
He is called the God of the whole
earth.

The Lord wants us to sing to the situations we face. We prophecy to our problems by speaking life into dead things "and call those things which do not exist as though they did." (Romans 4:17) The church is being revived as we prophecy life into our dead hopes and dreams. God has not forgotten His promises to us. He is restoring what has been stolen by the enemy. In this atmosphere of praise, we are decreeing that life comes back to the dry bones, and that God is raising up an army of end-time believers who will sing into existence the things that are going to come to pass. That the tent pegs of our sphere of influence are being lengthened and we are moving in an anointing that will break yokes of bondage and set the captives free. We are moving into a season where we must proclaim the victory and decree that we are entering into a place of fulfillment and joy. It's time to recapture what was ours and proclaim that we are able to take back what the enemy meant for evil and see it turned around for God's redemptive purposes.

Recently, I watched Sid Roth's show, *It's Supernatural on TV*. John Waller, who sang the featured song for the movie, "Fireproof", and was a guest on the show, has released a CD. He actually does spiritual warfare while singing. For example, he sings telling fear to leave. He also commands the blessings and sings blessings over his family. Apparently a lot of people have been delivered and healed while listening to the CD.

We are going to be singing the promises and praying in the Holy Ghost in order to see the fulfillment of our promises in the days ahead. Warfare prayers that include our prophetic promises, intercession, and praying the scriptures will prove to be effective weapons that drive back the enemy and keep him from advancing. The dynamic combination of praise, prayer, and proclamation usher in great power in the life of believers. It will release a surge of dominion power that will cause the heavens to rend and demons to flee. Strongholds are shattered that dispel bondages. The foothold of the enemy is demolished and any further attacks are stopped. When we employ the weapon of militant praise, we literally cause the enemy's camp to quake and reek destruction to his plans to rob, kill, and destroy.

Randy DeMain in his book *Dominion Surges* put into action the strategy of employing praise, proclamations, and decrees. As a result, his church, Amazing Grace Bible Fellowship grew and they went from one service to two. They also moved to a larger facility where it continues to be a lighthouse of praise in the community.

Randy's hometown, Redmond, Oregon experienced transformation to the point where other churches were also growing. Places of illicit activities went out of business. Many were being saved and coming to the Lord. Breakthrough happens when we persist in taking back enemy territory. We make a demand in the spirit realm and keep applying pressure to blast open areas of resistance. By speaking to the mountains of doubt and unbelief, we remove hindrances that block our destiny from being fulfilled.

Worship and warfare are a natural combination that break open the spirit realm. God has given us the key of David to unlock the realm of the spirit and to bind the rulers and principalities of darkness. This key speaks of spiritual authority which has been given to us, and as we use this key, we break through the spirit realm and stake our claim to what rightfully belongs to us. Worship is a major weapon that locks and unlocks the heavens.

Revelation 3:7 talks about the key of David stating, "These things says He who is holy, He who is true, He who has the key of David, He who opens and no one shuts and shuts and no one opens."

David Swan in his book *The Power of Prophetic Worship* explains that the application of this key through prophetic praise and worship releases the anointing of the spirit to drive off demonic powers, destroy strongholds, and create an open heaven.[2]

The act of seeking is a part of worship. The key to being a true worshipper is to seek His face. If we honor Him, God will honor us. As we put His kingdom and His priorities first, He will move mountains for us. We need only to listen to His voice to gain strategy. God will reveal Himself to those whose walks are upright and give revelation to bear up under pressure.

Like David, we must inquire of the Lord on how to wage war. At Ziklag, David conquered the Amalekites, as he strengthened his faith, put on the ephod, and sought the Lord's counsel. Ziklag was burned with fire, and David's two wives were taken captive. What looked hopeless was turned around as God assured David that not only would he overtake the Amalekites, but that he would without fail, recover all. (1 Samuel 30:8).

Worship always prepares the way for victory. The word Judah means praise, and the tribe of Judah led the procession when fighting the enemies of Israel. Fighting the good

---

2   David Swan, *The Power of Prophetic Worship*, Kuala Lumpur, Malaysia, Tan Suan Chew (David Swan) 2001.

fight of faith means we must be armed and ready to enter into the promises of God. We take hold of our destiny, come up to His holy hill of praise and speak to any mountains of doubt and fear to move out of the way and be cast into the sea, never to be seen again. God desires a warring church, with no one left on the sidelines. The bold confession of a warring child of God defeats the enemies' wiles when worship comes on the scene because it brings the enemy camp into confusion and causes division in the ranks.

TRIALS, TESTS AND
TESTIMONIES

Jehoshaphat was facing a multitude of armies coming against the Israelites, in 2 Chronicles 20. The Moabites, the Ammonites, and the inhabitants of Mount Seir were threatening annihilation. Jehoshaphat sought the Lord and proclaimed a fast throughout the land. The Lord told the Israelites to take their positions and He would fight the battle. Jehoshaphat appointed singers to sing and praise the Lord in their priestly garment, as they went out before the army. When they began to sing, the Lord set ambushes against the enemies and they began to self-slaughter.

After this, there was so much spoil, it took the Israelites three days to gather it all. So when we worship, we enter into the enemy's camp and cause destruction. Worship prepares us to enter into all that He has promised. It positions us to receive the anointing, that breaks yokes of bondage and sets the captives free. The battle precedes the victory. It takes a persevering spirit to enter into all that is promised, but as we stay filled with the spirit, we can overcome what was meant for evil and see it turned around for good. Afterwards, the spoils of war come when we keep a good attitude and remain faithful.

In 1 Samuel 17:46 David came against the Philistine giant, Goliath, and prophecies what will come to pass. He decrees, "This day the Lord will deliver you into my hand, and I will strike you and take your head from you. And this day I will give the carcasses of the camp of the Philistines to the birds of the air and the wild beasts of the earth, that all the earth may know that there is a God in Israel. Verse 47 continues by saying, "Then all this assembly shall know that the Lord does not save with sword or spear; for the battle *is* the Lord's, and He will give you into our hands."

Sure enough, David defeated Goliath, cut off his head and used Goliath's head as a trophy. Jessie Duplantis, in his tape series *Close Encounters of the God Kind,* says that David showed us how to get ahead in life. We make headway as we take back ground from the enemy by refusing to be moved by circumstances. An attack is launched by using the weapons He has placed in our hands. The weapons of our warfare are not carnal. This may mean moving in love toward offenders, and not allowing an offense to take hold. We are then rewarded for not giving up and allowing God to fight on our behalf. Honor and favor are in store for the faithful. When the enemy comes in like a flood, the Spirit of the Lord will lift up a standard against him (Isaiah 59:19).

Jesus won the battle for us against sin, and after He suffered on the cross, Colossians 2:15 states, "Having disarmed principalities and powers, He made a public spectacle of them, triumphing over them in it."

We are not forgotten. Just as Joseph learned to forgive his brothers from selling him into slavery and throwing him into a pit, we must keep ourselves from bitterness toward our offenders. When times of testing come, we must not give up. By not allowing circumstances to move us out of God's will, we keep the faith in spite of adverse conditions. The end result will make it all worthwhile. We need to keep a long-term vision. God has a plan to bring us into fruitfulness and healing. As we see God's intervention, we have a testimony (a trophy of grace) of God's faithfulness. We recount what Jesus has done in our lives and how we first came to believe.

There is no testimony without a test, no message without a mess. Trials reveal the heart of a man, but through testing, the heart undergoes transformation. Through the Great Physician's hand, healing occurs as the impurities are wiped clean. The surgeon works to remove the blockages that have formed over the years. Once the blood flow is restored, the person not only feels better but has also more stamina. Many times deliverance is needed for the person to be made whole.

When we go through trials, God wants us to be assured that the testing of our faith produces patience. James says,

"But let patience have it's perfect work, that you be perfect and complete, lacking nothing." We grow in grace as we allow our faith to be stretched so we can reach full stature. Testing precedes promotion. We are being positioned to enter into everything that He promised.

Revelation 12:11 states, "And they overcame him by the blood of the Lamb and by the word of their testimony, and they did not love their lives to the death."

Worship acknowledges God's sovereignty over all. It brings a blessing and causes us to focus on the goodness of God. When we give God our sacrifice of praise, we allow Him to change our priorities and to bring us into the fullness of His presence where our joy can be restored. The Bible says to put on the garment of praise for the spirit of heaviness (Isaiah 61:3).

Morning and evening, we need to praise and worship the Lord because when we do, we allow His glory to come down in our midst. When His glory comes on the scene, miracles happen. We are swept into a wave of thunderous praise that brings deliverance and healing.

Many in the last days will see His hand operating in their midst, but there must be a yielding of the heart so He can restore what the enemy has tried to rob. When the heart is yielded, God can move unhindered to restore the brokenhearted and bind up their wounds. It takes a contrite heart that allows God to prune back the branches so fruitfulness occurs. Many have been tried and tested, but there will be a day of reaping the fruit of faithfulness, so remain steadfast and keep your faith. Though it be tested, it is more precious than gold. So stay fixed on the goal and don't allow the enemy to steal your joy. The joy of the Lord is your strength (Nehemiah 8:10). Praise enables you to recapture joy that has been stolen, so you can be taken to a place of healing. Don't grow weary in well-doing for you shall reap if you don't give up. The season of change is coming, and God's people will be taken to places of recompense and healing, because God's word is true and He is working to see you restored so you can be a blessing to others.

David experienced recovery and breakthrough in His life because He refused to break down or back down. He knew his day was coming when He would become king, but he refused to let others deter his destiny. Although he was anointed as king, it would be several years before he would take the throne. In the meantime, King Saul was after him, trying to kill him due to jealousy. However, David learned patience through what he suffered, and his preparation period caused him to rely on the Lord and not lean on his own understanding. For the battles of this life are nothing compared to the glory that will be revealed in us. Jesus is the lion of the tribe of Judah who roars with victory. He has won the war and is fashioning us into warriors that shout with the voice of triumph… "We are more than conquerors through Him who loved us." (Romans 8:37)

PART II

THE TABERNACLE
OF DAVID

With the anointing of David as king of Israel, a new era is born. David was a man after God's own heart; he knew how to worship the Lord "in spirit and truth" (John 4:24). There was only one period in history where Israel dominated everything. It was under the reign of King David. David undergirded everything with praise and worship, which allowed him to bear up under it all. God perfected his character through trials and testings. By standing strong in his tests, David was shaped into a valiant warrior with whom God found favor. David pursued the Lord wholeheartedly and determined to seek His ways. His desire to please the Lord fueled his passion to build a house for Him. As he persisted in building a house of praise, David ushered in the glory of God.

David set up patterns of worship according to the directions he received from the Lord. Prior to David's reign, Mosaic worship consisted primarily of animal sacrifices, prayers, intercession, and the high priest alone approached the ark. There was no development of the arts or creativity with the exception of the craftsmanship of the tabernacle and furnishings. David's relationship with God was directed toward the tabernacle where the ark of the covenant lay. During David's lifetime, the Tabernacle was where worship occurred. God gave Moses specific instructions for building the Tabernacle and the ark of the covenant in the book of Exodus.

The ark of the covenant was the most sacred of all the furniture in the Tabernacle. It housed the Ten Commandments, manna, and Aaron's (the high priest's) rod. The Israelites often carried it into battle with them because it signified the presence of God.

The Tabernacle was a portable tent with a wooden framework that gave it stability. It consisted of three main areas.

The outer court could be accessed by any Israelite, as long as they were ritually clean. However, the people were not allowed to go any further into the Tabernacle. The first chamber, the Holy Place could only be accessed by the Levite Priests. It was here that the priests ministered to God daily, but not without first washing their hands and feet in the laver. They had to be consecrated unto the Lord to perform their sacred tasks.

The Holy of Holies, the innermost chamber, was where the Ark of the Covenant and the Mercy Seat lay. A curtain, known as the "veil", separated the Holy Place from the Most Holy place (Holy of Holies.) It was made of fine linen and blue, purple and scarlet yarn. There were pictures of cherubim (angels) embroidered onto it. Cherubim are involved in the worship and praise of God. They are guardians attached to the throne of God as a protective barrier to guard His holiness. The tabernacle contains many representations of cherubim. It is interesting to note that the cherubim stopped Adam from reentering the Garden of Eden, after the fall. The flaming sword that turned every way indicated a supernatural boundary, that prevented him access to the Tree of Life, so he would not live forever in his fallen state.

In the same way the veil, served as a barrier to prevent man from approaching a holy God. Only the high priest was authorized to go behind the veil. On Yom Kippur, the Day of Atonement, he went in to make atonement for the sins of the people that they committed for the past year. Again it was the blood of bulls and goats that were sacrificed as an offering to the Lord.

Later David built a tent for the Lord that was open on all sides. Walls were no longer needed, nor a holy of holies. Yet the Kabod, weightiness of the Lord rested on the Mercy Seat because the Levite priests continued to consecrate themselves to the Lord. They understood the importance of keeping the flame burning on the altar, so that the manifest presence of the Lord would dwell there continuously.

ENTERING THE SECRET PLACE

We can be around the things of God, but unless we enter into pure undefiled intimacy with the Lord, we remain in the outer court. It's like being an outsider looking in. We must begin to ascend into the holy of holies. We enter in by the blood of the Lamb. No other sacrifice will do. When Jesus went to the cross, He ripped the veil that separated man from God because of sin. Now we are free to worship God because we have a new and living way.

In the Mosaic order, the blood of bulls and goats allowed entrance. But now we gain entrance through an intimate relationship with the Lord Jesus. Worship allows us to touch the hem of His garment. We press through the narrow place until we see Jesus high and lifted up. He regards our worship as sweet sacrifice, and we are taken up with Him into the holy of holies. Our worship allows us to enter into a more intimate relationship with Him.

We demonstrate that He is Lord of our lives, by keeping His commands. As we stay connected to God and His word, an increase in anointing and power will result. However, we must count the cost. Many will fall asleep during these end times; we must stay awake. A slumbering, apathetic spirit will try to infiltrate many of God's people, but we must pray in the Holy Ghost and keep ourselves filled with the Spirit. Cry out to the Father for a fresh, new infilling of His spirit. As we keep a full tank of the Spirit, we are empowered from on high to do His work. It's going to get darker out there, so we need to stay refueled and on fire for the Lord. It's time for the people of God to rise up and decree that worship is leading the way and that order is being perfected out of chaos.

David not only changed the tabernacle, but he also brought a new way of worship that ushered in healing, restoration, and breakthrough. As we worship "in spirit and truth" (John 4:24), we avail ourselves to God's spirit and as we allow His spirit to encompass us, we become filled with His presence. His presence brings joy. The spirit brings peace and relief from burdens, for as we worship, His presence fills the temple. We become the tabernacle that God inhabits. All that worship according to this pattern will find that they are participating in God's divine order.

David set the order of worship for us. Davidic worship is the prototype of modern-day worship. David brought the ark of the covenant back to Jerusalem after it was captured by the Philistines. The Ark that symbolized the very presence of God was now back in the midst of the people in Jerusalem. Psalm 24 depicts the celebration of the ark being brought back from captivity. David sang, "Open up the gates and let the King of Glory come in."

There was food, singing, and playing of instruments. David danced with all his might before the Lord. As the ark entered the City of David, David placed it in a tent, the tabernacle of David. Michal (Saul's daughter) saw David dancing and whirling before the Lord. She reprimanded David for uncovering himself in the site of the eyes of the maids of his servants.

David responded that he would get even more undignified than this. (2 Samuel 6:14-22)

It reminds me of the clash of the spirit with the law. Jesus rebuked the Pharisees because they would tithe but neglect justice, mercy, and faith. It was about doing the right thing outwardly but ignoring the weightier issues. Thus, Michal's concern centered around how things looked to outsiders. This stifles the spirit because to worship "in spirit and truth" (John 4:24) requires an abandonment of oneself to the Lord, and He becomes our sole focus.

Bear in mind however, that Jesus did not come to abolish the law (tithing), but rather He came to fulfill it. (Matthew 5:17) Therefore Christ fulfills the law.

Michal presents a critical, religious spirit that will try to quench worship saying, "You are making a fool of yourself. What will people think?"

The devil hates us worshipping Abba and will try to stop it at all costs. Praise can vanquish any enemy that Satan uses. It is interesting to note that the scriptures say that Michal remained barren to the day of her death. Lack of praise causes us to remain like a stagnant stream, no overflowing results in focusing on ourselves and keeps us joyless. We stay watered as we praise Him, for in our praise, we access His throne room and enter into the holy of holies because we are consumed by His love. No other lover will do; we are moved by His love to enter into the place of holy matrimony. We stay mesmerized by His presence as we lock eyes with Him in His chamber. We are His bride, and we need His presence to completely fill us until we can no longer stand. We come to Him through His blood sacrifice, and we leave knowing He is our heavenly bridegroom. But if we will linger in His presence, we will see Him in all His glory. The Lord wants us to remain with Him in the hidden place so He can reveal mysteries so profound that we are in awe of Him. We are being taken on a divine journey to the throne room, where His presence ushers us into the Holy of Holies. God will bring us to this place of glory, as we stay with Him and press through, into His chamber, so we are transformed and molded into His image. We are created for praise and as we allow praise to have its way in our lives, we are completely taken over by His spirit. This brings divine revelation (wisdom) so we are enabled to accomplish His purposes for our lives.

Many times, we are rushed and give God crumbs of worship, but to enter into the fullness of His glory, we must allow Him time to move in our temple, so we become carriers of the flame of His love. His love is what changes us, from glory to glory. So as we linger in His presence, we are becoming the tabernacle of David on the earth today. God wants the body to be built up in their most holy faith, in order to experience the manifestation of His glory in the end times. He desires His bride to be partakers of His end time plan to cover the earth with His glory, and to be a light to those who are in darkness.

Worship allows God's presence to infiltrate the darkness, so that a manifestation of His power and majesty can be seen. God is raising up the tabernacle of David to usher in the outpouring of the Holy Spirit in the last days.

We can find God's style of worship within its borders. To begin, the tabernacle was uncomplicated in its design, but mighty in purpose. The tabernacle lasted for thirty three years. This time frame replicates the life span of Christ. Jesus lived thirty three years, glorifying God while being fully incarnate. He wants us to discover the ancient path that unlocks the key of David.

The Prophecy Of Amos

Amos 9:11–12 states, "On that day I will raise up the Tabernacle of David, which has fallen down, and repair its damages, I will raise up its ruins and rebuild it as in the days of old, that they may possess the remnant of Edom, and all the Gentiles who are called by My name."

Worship precedes revival and when tabernacle of David worship becomes prevalent it releases the fullness of destiny. Worship activates the Davidic Kingdom (Jewish people, Israel) and causes it to be restored, because the activation brings healing of the nations. Jeremiah prophesied spiritual restoration of Israel through a national revival (Jeremiah 31:31–37). Jeremiah speaks about the New Covenant and proceeds to prophesy that from the least of them to the greatest of them, a sweeping spiritual transformation will touch the entire nation. Thus Israel will be restored and its remnant will inherit the promises of Abraham. This will trigger the full measure of the Gentiles (all nations) to come in and be saved because the blessing has been released for the harvest of nations and the outpouring of the Holy Spirit.

Israel's restoration has begun with the migration of the Jews back to the Holy Land.

One of the organizations that has been instrumental in supporting Israel, and sending Jews back to Israel, is the International Fellowship of Christians and Jews. Their program, On Wings of Eagles is helping Jewish people realize their dream of living in Israel, while at the same time fulfilling Bible prophecy.

Ezekiel 37:12-14 pronounces:

> "Therefore prophesy and say to them, "Thus says the Lord God." Behold O My people, I will open your graves and cause you to come up from your graves, and bring you into the land of Israel.
>
> "Then shall you know that I am the Lord, when I have opened your graves, O My people, and brought you up from your graves."
>
> "I will put My Spirit in you, and you shall live, and I will place you in your own land. Then you shall know that I the Lord, have spoken it and performed it," says the Lord."

David Herzog in his book, *Glory Invasion, Walking Under An Open Heaven* states, "I believe that as soon as the remnant of God's chosen people goes to Israel, their homeland, God will start to breathe His spirit upon them and bring national revival. This in turn will cause global revival."[3]

---

[3]   David Herzog, *Glory Invasion, Walking Under an Open Heaven*, Shippensburg, PA. Destiny Image Publishers. 2012.

As the Jews return to Israel, a mighty outpouring of the Holy Spirit will occur, as the entire root becomes planted in the land, promised to their forefathers. When the people gather in Israel, the promises of Abraham will overtake them, and allow them to reap the benefits of the Abrahamic covenant. As the Jews settle there and give God the glory, He will cause them to be restored and walk in the promises. By preparing their hearts, they will see God's hand move on the land and bring prosperity. It's a time to gather all the nations, and to bring in the harvest of souls. When the full measure of Jews arrive in Israel to make Aliyah (Jews immigrating to Israel. Aliyah means ascent or "going up"), a mighty move of the spirit will trigger revival. This in turn will cause a global shift that will usher in the greatest outpouring of the Spirit since the early 1900's.

So, as Israel becomes revived, the nations shall reap the benefits of her healing harvest. It's as if she has been restored from the dead, and brought back to life. The restoration of Israel will bring a wave of global evangelism that will usher in such wonders and miracles, that it will be hailed as an invasion of His glory. Many of the Jews will be coming back to understand the roots of their faith, and acknowledge the truth about Jesus and His reason for coming. They will understand the Scriptural references to the second coming of Jesus and prepare for His return. There will be a national repentance of sin and many will seek God's face and call upon the Lord. Also there will be a

National Day of Prayer instituted that will sweep the globe and people will change and be restored, as a result of Israel's resurrection from the dead.

But to enter into the fullness of what Christ came to accomplish, we must pray for the Jewish state (people) and believe that salvation truly belongs to the Jew first (Romans 1:16). Thus the need not to exclude the Jews from hearing the gospel message. We must not desert the apple of His eye during Israel's travail and growing warfare with its enemies. They must see something different; the love of God demonstrated through action. Stepping out of our comfort zones, to reach the Jews will enable us to be lighthouses of hope in the end-time harvest.

We must pray for the peace of Jerusalem, and keep knocking until we see the fruits of our labor. Our labor is not in vain, for we are the city on the hill that cannot be hidden. Our light shines in the darkness and as we determine to stay filled with the Spirit, we touch the lives of those around us and bring the warmth of God's love and care. Those who speak His words and give testimony of His ways will be empowered by the Holy Spirit. "For it's not by might, nor by power, but by My Spirit, says the Lord." (Zechariah 4:6). Spirit-empowered words contain seeds that bring forth a harvest at the appointed time. When we speak words that magnify the Lord, we set into motion angels that work to bring the harvest in. They work in tandem with our words of faith to bring healing and protection from harm.

Co-Laboring With Angelic Hosts

Davidic Praise Worship releases sounds that activate heavenly beings to bring in the harvest of souls. Certain sounds unlock portals that have been closed in the spirit realm, so when angels hear the song of the Lord, they are commissioned to bring revival to the nations. Breakthrough angels are able to bring down strongholds as the Word of the Lord is spoken and faith is released. Faith is the substance that releases the angelic beings to bring in the harvest. As we keep our faith intact in tough times, we are positioned to reach the lost and bear good fruit. Matthew 13:41 states, "The Son of Man will send forth his angels and they will gather out of His kingdom all things that offend,and those who practice lawlessness."

In the end times there will be a great harvest of souls, but to enter in, there must be a new sound that releases the resources of heaven to bring about a mighty outpouring of the spirit.

John reports in Revelation 14:6, "Then I saw another angel flying in the midst of heaven, having the everlasting gospel to preach to those who dwell on the earth-to every nation, tribe, tongue and people, saying with a loud voice, "Fear God and give glory to Him, for the hour of His judgment has come; and worship Him who made heaven and earth, the sea and the springs of water."

By co-laboring with the angelic hosts, we allow God's purposes to come to pass. We petition heaven for an outpouring of God's spirit, while praising Him and asking Him to send forth His angels that gather. The gathering angels work to bring forth the harvest.

Mark 13:27 states, "And then He will send His angels and gather together His elect from the four winds, from the farthest part of earth to the farthest part of heaven."

God's spirit infiltrates enemy territory that was previously impenetrable, when we take our stand on the wall and intercede for our nation. There will be great revival in our nation, but we must stay on fire and carry the torch in spite of circumstances that are going on at the time. The times ahead will be perilous. We are the ones who will bring His word to a world that has spun out of control. We must keep our hearts from being overcharged; lest we fall away. Preparation is necessary, for it's becoming darker. So, as we endeavor to speak words that will encourage others, we are able to be a light in a dark world. We will be recognized by our love, so we need to stay connected to the Lord and be ready to give an account for what we believe.

We are now in a time where people are losing their jobs, and unemployment is at an all-time high. Many fear their future prospects, as well as an economy that has forced many to go on government assistance. The end-time harvest will bring a revival of enormous proportions, and many will seek the Lord as the times get more desperate. We must go to God as our high tower and seek refuge from the storms of life. As the tides rise and the waves crash around us, we must stay focused on the Lord. He is coming soon, and He wants us to be unafraid and trusting His purposes for our lives. When we take His words seriously and prepare, we are equipped to handle all that will transpire. But we must come up higher in our devotion to Him and believe that Jesus is able to bring relief and calm the storm. He wants us to rely on His report and to worship Him in all His glory. God is able to replace our sorrow with joy and bring beauty out of ashes. We are able to enter into worship as we bring Him all our concerns and leave them at His feet. This enables us to rise above all distractions and to enter into a place of rest. We are His dwelling place as we stand in the evil day and declare that God is making a way through the wilderness and restoring His order in our midst. He desires a remnant that will worship Him in the midst of chaos, so His order can come forth in the dark times.

Sparking Revival Of
The Nations

Although it's been said that revival is coming soon, the new wine always comes for the ones who wait in anticipation for it. The best wine is for the latter rain church. Latter rain refers to the end times outpouring of the Holy Spirit. Just as it was in the day of Pentecost, so the rain of the spirit is coming again, to bring a fire that cannot be extinguished. Revival winds are blowing as we allow worship to usher in a new wave of His spirit, that brings refreshing and healing. Worship facilitates revival as we seek His face and allow His presence to saturate our lives and bring a release of His glory. The Lord's presence comes when we seek Him wholeheartedly and take the time to come into His presence.

The Israelites understood that in order to please God, a sacrifice must be offered. The sacrifice that God accepts is that of a broken, contrite heart before Him. By pouring out our praise in response to God's goodness we are bringing Him a sacrifice of praise that will change the atmosphere of our hearts. When we seek Him with our whole heart we will find Him in all His glory. The glory realm demands that we praise Him without reservation, for as we seek to find Him, we are transported to the throne room, where He communes with us.

Whereas the tabernacle of Moses was for the Israelites alone, the tabernacle of David included both Jew and Gentile. Now, the church is the believing remnant. According to Revelation 5:9–10, this remnant of believers shall stand before the throne of God singing new songs and playing instruments as they collectively worship Jesus after the order of David's Tabernacle.[4]

As the prophecy is fulfilled, (Amos 9:11-12), the "One New Man" will emerge. Jew and Gentile alike will partake of His glorious riches as they sing praise and honor to Him who sits on the throne.

Ephesians 2:14–15, 22 says, "For He Himself is our peace who has made both Jew and Gentile one, and has broken down the middle wall of separation…to create in Himself one new man…in whom you also are being built together for a dwelling place of God in the Spirit."

At first only Jews were part of the church, but later the Gentiles were included. In fact the prophecy by Amos of a Gentile revival after Israel was restored was the motivator

---

4   Shane Warren Ministries, 2012. Shane Warren, *Secrets of the Well.* West Monroe, LA. Shane Warren Ministries, 2009.

to convince the apostles at the Jerusalem council to evangelize the Gentiles.

However, a spiritual blindness has fallen upon much of Israel that has prevented the Jews from entering into a personal relationship with Jesus.

According to Rms.11:25, the Jews rejection is temporary. Once the fullness of the Gentiles comes to put their trust in Christ, many of the Jews will be saved.

There is no division in Christ. Jesus has broken down the middle wall and reconciled man to himself. Jew and Gentile alike are made one in Christ.

The worship that will typify the "One New Man" can be seen in Revelation 15:3, which is the mixture of both old and new covenants. The song of Moses (Jewish) has become the marriage supper of the lamb (Christian).

The combined sounds release a prophetic flow of intercessory prayers that bring healing to the nations. Once this combination is allowed to permeate the atmosphere, the presence and glory of the Lord is manifested. Messianic music represents the best of both worlds. It bridges the gap between both camps and sparks revival. When the fullness of the old and the new is released, the glory of the Lord is seen.

When the "One New Man" operates in Davidic worship, heaven is rendered open. The veil is lifted and the rain of His glory shows up. He stands in golden glory, and He desires that His people worship according to the pattern shown to David on the mountain. For when this pattern is followed, a release of His signs, wonders, and miracles follow. It's a now season to bring in the harvest and to see His hand move in the assembly.

This type of worship emulates heavenly patterns of worship around the throne room.

God is synchronizing heaven and earth at this time. When heaven and earth align, a mighty outpouring of the spirit will emerge. The rivers of revival are emerging as we worship according to His pattern. He is bringing the sound of mighty waterfalls and great thundering to shake the foundations. The sound of many waters will be heard in the church.

My friend Chris Zimmerman Machado recently read Amos 9:11 in the Ignite Church located in West Haven, Connecticut. She is a prophetic intercessor.

God gave her a vision of New England, and she saw a tent over the land that was fallen down. Then Mike Smith, the worship leader and pastor took a giant pole, and he hoisted up the tent. Chris said that God will use Mike to lift up David's fallen tent. And he is raising people up all over New England to fulfill this prophecy. It's the high praises that will change the temperature of New England and cause its waste places to be rebuilt.

In fact, a direct result of this prophecy being fulfilled will be the activation of David's throne being restored. Jesus will come to rule on the throne of David because Davidic worship is the key that unlocks this ancient prophecy. Thus, the throne of David will be established and his former glory will be restored. 2 Samuel 7:16 highlights God's covenant with David, which states, "And your house and your kingdom shall be established forever before you. Your throne shall be established forever."

On the day of Pentecost, Peter reiterates God's promise to David in Acts 2:30 stating, "Therefore being a prophet and knowing that God had sworn with an oath to him that of the fruit of his body, according to the flesh, He would raise up the Christ to sit on his throne."

Many want revival, but few are willing to pay the price to see it manifest. There must be a rendering of the heart to God and a turning away from sin. Repentance is essential to receiving the healing of the nations.

We need to rediscover what the spirit is saying to the church in the last days. It will be times of great darkness, but the gospel will go forth as those who are called by God's name begin to petition heaven, humble themselves, and seek His face. Then shall they hear from heaven as they repent of the nation's sin. This will cause them to be established and enable the hand of God to move on the nation's behalf.

Those who are called by His name are the believing remnant and those who will usher in His spirit. The way is up, and the time is now. So we must keep ourselves stirred up in His spirit and allow the Spirit to bring healing to our tabernacles so we can share in His holiness. In this way, we are able to bring Him glory and be His representatives on the earth.

It's time to keep ourselves in God's love because as we do, we are enabled to be the living, breathing manifestation of God's glory. We know that we are able to walk in divine love as we take up our crosses and follow Him. It's in following Him, that we give up our lives. But in relinquishment we find our lives, and experience meaning and true purpose. Before Adam was, Jesus was. He knows that we are His bride as we take Him at His word and believe His promises. For in the end times we must believe that God is watching over us and His will is for our growth and expansion. (Jeremiah 29:11)

As we face the giants in our land, His word illuminates our path bringing healing and refreshment from life's pressures. We must contend for the faith!

Now, is the time to preach and teach the word in season and out of season. When our lives are pleasing to Him, we enter into a whole new dimension of life, and are able to enjoy the peace and prosperity Jesus died to give us

God is the wind beneath our wings. He enjoys our worship and is moved by a broken and contrite heart. He knows the path we take, and as we allow Him to break our hearts with the things that break His heart, then we are able to be used to repair and restore. Because as we give up what we want in favor of what God desires, then we are ready to partake in His perfect plan, because of our willingness to obey and seek His face.

Davidic worship allows us to experience the fullness of what God intended for man before the foundations of the world. The glory zone keeps us in awe of Him, as we gaze upon His majesty. It's the high praises of God's people that will usher in a new wave of His glory. Let's ascend up the holy mountain of praise so we can magnify His name!

FEATURES OF
DAVIDIC WORSHIP

One of the first features of Davidic worship is the raising of the intensity level of the worship. It's hot, hot, hot. When I inquired of the Lord what this worship looks like, I saw a man bowing and swinging his arms up and down and moving his legs in unison. He was dancing before the Lord and giving Him praise. Immediately I knew in my spirit it was David. It's fervent prayer and fasting that will allow our spirit to enter into this new level of worship. The new song will set the gold standard for entering into this move of the spirit.

Tehillah means to sing a song of praise that is spontaneous. It is from the heart and has never been sung before. Both the words and melody are spontaneously created. This song it can be in tongues or in one's native language. It allows a person to be swept up in heavenly worship, because as we worship in spirit and in truth, we capture heaven's sounds; and in doing so, we literally bring heaven to earth. The Lord may also "download" a song or melody to us during worship, and as we sing it back to him, we experience His powerful presence. Prophetic songs are able to breakthrough areas of resistance in a believer's life. They carry within them an anointing to break yokes and remove strongholds. The song of the Lord has great power to cause eruptions in the spiritual realm. It has the ability to stop evil from advancing and to bring down enemy ploys. When we sing in the spirit, we join with our heavenly hosts to see the victory enforced ahead of time! God's spirit is able to gain control, as we enter into extended times of worship. Spirit led worship propels us into the very throne room of God.

Allowing the Holy Spirit room to move in our worship services is of the utmost importance. By staying unencumbered by life's circumstances, we are able to enter into a place where we can hear God speak. As we worship in this new way, we are drawing on heaven's resources. Angels are attracted to worship and come into the service for ministry purposes. Even Jesus comes on the scene because He says, "Where two or three are gathered then I am in the midst of them." (Matthew 18:20). His enthroned responses can take the form of prophecy, healings, miracles, and speaking to hearts, a call to silence and awe, conviction of sin, and salvation of sinners.

A second characteristic of Davidic worship is worship through song and instrument day and night. The 24-7 worship is spreading through the world. Mike Bickle of Kansas is leading the charge with the House of Prayer (IHOP).

It is based on Revelation 4:5 harp and bowl worship around the throne room.

Now when he had taken the scroll, the four living creatures and the twenty-four elders fell down before the Lamb, each having a harp, and golden bowls full of incense, which are the prayers of the saints (Revelation 5:8). The harp represents worship, and the golden bowl symbolizes prayer and intercession.

Intercession and prayer can be difficult at times but when mixed with spontaneous worship, and high praise, the flow of the Spirit is released. When praise is accompanied by fasting, giving, worship and proclamation, a greater measure of the Spirit is accessed. When the Spirit is allowed free reign, the power to manifest miracles and signs is made more readily available.

The tabernacle of David was a place of unceasing prayer, praise, and proclamation. David appointed twenty-four groups of twelve musicians (a total of 880) who were set apart for prophetic worship. Also some sixteen ministries were called to perform twenty-four hours a day, seven days a week. Major revivals in the Old Testament were accompanied with Davidic worship. God's glory covered the tabernacle with a cloud by day and fire by night.

A great revival in Ireland was sparked by St. Patrick. It is noted that Patrick and his companions came down to a valley in the north of county Down, where they spotted a heavenly light and then heard the voice of angels, the sound of the heavenly choir. They called this place "Vallis Angelorum," the Valley of the Angels.

Bangor in Ireland was established by St. Comgall in Vallis Angelorum. This was the very ground where the heavenly angels appeared. Bangor became one of the most renowned centers of Celtic Christianity. Comgall planted the longest running 365, twenty-four-hour, seven-day house of prayer and worship since the tabernacle of David some three hundred years. Like the Moravians who came after them, they believed that the fire on the altar must never go out.

This strategic plan of twenty-four-hour–a–day prayer and worship created the most successful missionary expedition in church history. Large numbers of people went out and established allied churches all over Europe. The church plantings went as far as Russian and Bulgaria. Even after the Vikings invaded Ireland and took the Irish women as slaves, revival and transformation continued. The Irish women influenced the brutish pirates and won them over to Christianity.

Forerunners are now pushing through and creating open portals where the angels are ascending and descending, where heaven is heard and seen. Open heaven experiences include visions, dreams, and visitations. God is not limited by our five senses. He wants us to expect Him to move in new ways, which will spark revival. He desires to release the floodgates of revelation so we can move into the new thing He has in store for us. Nothing will be withheld; everything is possible.

Only as we come into the place of intimacy can we reap the full measure of our destiny. He holds the keys, and as we inquire as to what He has in store for us, then we are able to access portals of wisdom that He has laid up for us. We need only to come up to meet Him. The invitation is to come.

God is enthroned in the praises of His people. He releases the new song when we when we bring Him the best we have to offer. Just as a greeting card expresses the sentiments of the sender, a card that is from the heart, a homemade card is all the more special. It carries an individualized message that is truly memorable. By singing melodies to the Lord we send our heavenly Bridegroom a love letter that pierces the darkness. So as we sing a new song to the Lord, we express our devotion and offer up a sacrifice of praise!

Julie True is one who recognizes and responds to the sounds of heaven. She sings verses from the Psalms, adding spontaneous worship, to create an atmosphere conducive to healing and relief from demonic oppression.

God responds to a heart that is bent on seeking Him and not letting go until we hear from heaven. This brings Him great glory because He is waiting on us to capture His heart. He delights in our willingness to press through into the glory zone. It takes a close relationship with the Father to bring us into the place of intimacy, but there is a price to pay to carry the anointing of the Lord. We must not handle the things of God lightly but we must reverence His presence and be a keeper of the flame. Will you be a carrier of His glory to the nations?

The third feature of Davidic worship is that it's instrumental in nature. Psalm 150 instructs us to praise the Lord with different musical instruments. God likes variety, in creation and also in the expression of music. King David enjoyed the complexity of different arrangements of music and knew what instruments to play for the best sound possible. Likewise, certain songs have different degrees of anointing based on the instruments or the vocalists involved. David understood the importance of appointing skilled singers and instrumentalists based on their specific anointing.

The Psalms were first introduced out of David's tabernacle. In the Psalms (a musical book), three individuals stand out: Heman, Asaph, and Jeduthun. These three men were the main leaders of the Levitical ensembles. Heman was the lead singer, Asaph was the choir director, and Jeduthun, also referred to as Ethan, was the musical director.

In the Psalms usually at the beginning of each chapter, is a short message that contains a name or a description. These headings pinpoint the type of sound that God likes in worship. For example, Psalm 4's heading is addressed to the Chief Musician. David instructs him to play the stringed instruments. The inscription reads, "The Safety of the Faithful, A Psalm of David." Certain songs carry an anointing that is best played in specific keys or with a particular instrument. Thus, each Psalm instructs the leaders what instrument to play to create the atmosphere of heaven. Thus it is imperative to seek God's blueprint prior to leading worship.

The new song (prophetic utterance) activates heavenly beings that keep the fire burning before the throne room and are able to detonate strongholds that keep the believer from breaking through. The end-time harvest is dependent on keeping the fire stoked within us, for as we keep ourselves on fire and in love with Jesus, we are enabled to be carriers of the flame of His glory. We are taken to a place of restoration as we become the flame that will burn continuously before the throne of grace. We are becoming more like Jesus as we stay filled with the Spirit and allow His ways to become our ways. He wants us to become like David where we have fervent love for one another and allow Him to burn off all that is not of Him.

As we do, we will be enabled to do great feats that will amaze and delight us. We are the champions that do battle with our Goliath's, and have overcome them, because "He who is in you is greater than he who is in the world" (1 John 4:4). Goliath was no match for David because David knew that his trust was in God alone and that God had already won the battle. Therefore, he had no reason to fear ("What can man do to me?"). The battle has been won in the spirit realm; we need only to access His power and glory through prophetic intercession and the high praises of God. In this way, we are able to engage the spirit realm and take back what the enemy has taken from us.

We are becoming more and more like Jesus as we come to the throne of grace and stay connected to His words. His words are becoming *rhema* when we speak them into existence and allow His voice to rule and reign in our lives. For just as David brought a whole new era of worship, as we allow ourselves to become instruments of praise, we access heavenly portals that are bound by the enemy. By singing a new song, we activate angelic hosts that do warfare in the heavenlies to release demonic strongholds.

David Herzog in his book, *Glory Invasion, Walking Under An Open Heaven* talks about preaching at a crusade in Africa where many people were in need of deliverance. In particular one woman who was demon possessed, started hissing like a cat while approaching the stage. David made a decision to keep worshipping rather than draw attention to the devil's antics. He began singing a new song. The words were, "In heaven's glory there are no demons or darkness. Your will be done on earth as it is in Heaven." As he began to sing he could see angels coming down upon the people from a portal in heaven. When he pointed in the direction where the angels were, mass deliverances were taking place as he sung. People fell on the floor, screaming, coughing and vomiting. Many were being set free from witchcraft, generational curses and freemasonry. The only problem was that the woman who was demon possessed was still manifesting. So, David asked the angels to accompany and minister to this woman. She started to point to the angels on her right and left and she screamed in fear. However after she fell to the ground kicking and screaming she was gloriously set free and in her right mind. Many people were not only delivered but saved as people worshipped the Lord.

God uses the angels to dispel the darkness and cause demons to flee. As we sing a new song, we allow ourselves to labor with our heavenly hosts to bring down demonic entrapments set by the enemy. Praise stills the avenger. It activates angelic forces that war on our behalf.

We are being instructed to begin to war in the spirit realm when we enter enemy territory so we can enter into the new thing that God has purposed for us. The enemy desires to stop a new move of God. Hence, we must bring about heaven's resources to counter the attack. The Israelites understood this principle, by sending the singers out before the battle erupted. Prior to gaining new ground there is a warfare that takes place. The battle precedes the victory. We must use God's resources to cross over into our Promised Land.

Joshua saw Jericho fall, as he followed the pattern the Lord gave him. By walking around the city seven times, blowing the trumpets, and declaring the victory with a mighty shout, the walls of Jericho fell down. A battle cry (shout), caused the enemy to let go, because the sound caused an eruption in the heavenlies, releasing an enemy stronghold. The sound caused the enemy's camp to retreat and to quake before the Lord. So, as the new sound goes up, the enemy fortress comes down. By seeking God's face prior to the battle, we gain wisdom and insight on how to proceed. We must remain determined to stay connected to the Lord, to see His hand move on our behalf. The sounds of heaven are activated as we war in the spirit. God enjoys the complexity of sound. He wants us to speak to our destiny and to understand that our voice emits sound waves that activate realms in the spirit. Thus it is important to declare our prophetic promises that God has spoken to us. Our prophetic promises allow us to remain steadfast while waiting for their fulfillment. We also need to pray in the Spirit, to align our voice with His perfect will. This causes the Spirit to create the new thing, that God is doing.

There is a new work that God desires to do in His people. As we wait in faith, adding the prophetic song of the Lord we see God's hand move in the right timing. There is a link of the new thing that God is doing and the new song. Prior to a fresh move of the Spirit, a change in the atmosphere of the heavenlies is needed. To bring about the change, a shift occurs as the new song (sound) is activated. This sound produces warfare in the heavenlies and signals angelic hosts to work to see it manifested in the natural.

As God's presence hovers over our lives, the Man of War, fights for us and He makes the crooked places straight and leads the way into the new thing.

Isaiah 42:9-10 pronounces:

> Behold the former things have come to pass. And new things I declare.
> Before they spring forth I tell you of them,
> Sing to the Lord a new song. And His praise from the ends of the earth
> You who go down to the sea and all that is in it.
> Your coastlands and your inhabitants of them.

Interestingly enough, this song is participating in heaven's song by the spirit's enablement, a song described as the sound (voice) of many waters.

By singing in the spirit, we are actually causing disruption to the enemy's plans and causing peace to rule and reign. Staying filled with God's spirit, will enable us to release the Lord's song, which will bring rest to cope with life's pressures. We can ask the Lord for a new song that will encourage us in the midst of troubled times. We are able to impart a blessing to those in turmoil, as we allow Him to restore our soul and pray for His divine intervention and guidance. In turbulent times, we need to be able to keep ourselves calm and in faith, trusting that He is in control. In the last days, many will be seeking solace and need encouragement that only comes from a source of strength. God's peace will enable us to stand in the evil day and in turn offer relief to those who are hurting.

Other features of Davidic worship include outward actions such as bowing down, lifting the hands, clapping, or the festal shout.

Processions were common around festivals involving a pilgrimage to the sanctuary. The Ark was carried in procession usually accompanied by dance.

There might be a call to worship using trumpets or other instruments. Tambourines accompany the dancing, as well as other instruments of praise. Extended periods of praise amplified the anointing resulting in a climax when the word of the Lord came forth.

Seeking God's divine order became a necessary ingredient in God's presence being made manifest. When we extend our worship for an extra twenty minutes or so, it makes a big difference in the spiritual atmosphere.

The tabernacle of David's worship offers a model of recovering a sense of the Lord's presence with His people.

Finally, worshippers would pledge their allegiance to the Lord in some act of covenant renewal. They would give thanks and lift their hands as a sign of loyalty. Speaking words of commitment such as "You are my God" or "I am your servant" was common.

At the end of a time of worship, a blessing was pronounced over the worshippers. Speaking God's word over ourselves and others invokes God's blessing because God says His word does not return void. So when we speak to our circumstances, we are declaring that God is able to do what He has promised and bring about relief from the cares of this world. He is our El-Shaddai, our all sufficient one. In Jewish circles, it was common to recite the Aaronic blessing.

> The Lord bless you and keep you
> The Lord make His face shine upon you
> And be gracious to you;
> The Lord lift up His countenance upon you,
> And give you peace.

> Numbers 6:24–26

Conclusion

In summary, the keys to lead a lifestyle of Worship and Purpose are:

Enter into His courts with thanksgiving.

Thank the Lord for His goodness and mercy over your life. Praise Him for what He has done and what He is about to do in your life. Thank God before the battle is won. Take the time to reflect upon a time that the Lord spoke to you and gave you direction that resulted in a good outcome. Keep a gratitude journal and make regular entries. Listen for His voice and obey His promptings as He spurs you onto victory!

Pray the Scriptures

When we pray the Scriptures, we bring God's word to bear upon our circumstance. We allow His hand to bring it to pass by speaking it into existence. Isaiah 55:11 states, "So shall My word be that goes forth from My mouth;

It shall not return to Me void, but it shall accomplish what I please and it shall prosper in the thing for which I sent it."

In other words, as we take God's word (the Sword of the Spirit) to heart, we proclaim the victory and see God move on our behalf. We partner with God, as we allow His word to have its way in our lives.

For in the last days, there will be an outpouring of His spirit, that will bring healing, deliverance and great joy. But it will also be a time of great pressure and travail. As we speak to the mountains of despair and desperation to come down, we keep His words in our mouths and proclaim that He is our stronghold in the day of trouble.

In the article "The Even Better Way to Beat Stress" from *Women's World* magazine, it explains that praying the Scriptures out loud is a very powerful antidote to stress. Benefits of lowered stress lead to greater immunity from disease.

Researchers cite that "Psalms and prayers are written in a way that requires you to slow your breathing as you speak them, lowering your pulse and your blood pressure."[5]

By allowing God's spirit to take full residence in us, we become insulated from the stresses of this life. Praying in the Spirit (praying in tongues) allows us to remain at peace even in the midst of trying circumstances. Our God is a consuming fire, and as we yield the sword to do battle in the heavenly realm, we are surrounded by hordes and

---

5   Gabrielle Lichterman, *The Even Better Way to Beat Stress*. *Women's World*, Englewood Cliffs, New Jersey. April 15, 2013 issue.

hordes of angelic hosts who do battle in the heavenlies on our behalf. For as we yield the sword of the spirit, we proclaim the victory of The Lord Jesus Christ and His armies! It's going to get darker out, but as we speak out loud, to our destiny, we keep ourselves stirred up in the spirit and allow God's spirit to bring it to pass.

Worship Him in the Spirit.

Ephesians 5:18-20 exhorts us to "And do not be drunk with wine, in which is dissipation, but be filled with the Spirit,

Speaking to one another, in psalms and hymns and spiritual songs, singing and making melody in your heart to the Lord.

Giving thanks always for all things to God the Father in the name of our Lord, Jesus Christ."

Let your heart exude the melodies of your spirit. Maintain your zeal for the Lord and let the rivers of living water flow from within. Sing a new song, a song that is unrehearsed and spontaneous, for, as you sing a new song, you are bringing down strongholds in the spirit realm and activating angelic hosts to war on your behalf. Spontaneous worship changes the atmosphere and removes enemy entrapments. The enemy hates us worshipping Abba, but even more so, he hates spontaneous worship, because it causes him to be silenced and foils his plots. Praise carries the breaker anointing; that's why the Israelites sent Judah (praise) first before the battle.

Praise Jesus during the day.

When we praise God during the day, despite the situation, we are giving God the glory. As we bring God honor, we are able to rise above the circumstances and see things from His perspective. Praise brings hope, and hope does not disappoint us. We are bringing God's presence to bear upon the situation, so we can stay focused and lean on Him during trying times.

We are able to keep the faith, as we give Him our sacrifice of praise, and in turn, he takes our offering and turns it around for His glory. As Paul and Silas gave God the sacrifice of Praise while in jail, their chains came off, and they were set free!

Speaking God's promises over your life

Allow God to speak His promises to you and to give you clarity and favor to pursue your calling. Pray for His direction and guidance and wait on Him without wavering. Begin to keep a prayer journal and record what God is speaking to you, so you can know His perfect will. Once you discern His will, pray for Him to bring it to pass. Pray for wisdom and revelation and let God's word be your guiding light. Drink freely from the well of revelation, so you will become all that God has planned for you. He knew you before the foundations of the earth and has made provision for you. Come to Him and be transformed!

Encourage one Another in the Lord

We encourage one another in the Lord as we give ourselves fully to Him and prepare our vessel, to bring Him great glory. Praise lifts up our spirit, and as we live to be a blessing, we experience a greater dimension of grace and healing. As we stay in His presence, we are able to rise above the circumstances and gain wisdom to bear upon our problems. When we become stronger and more resilient, we are able to impart God's love and care to a lost and dying world. Healing comes through encouraging words spoken in truth. Pray for one another and stand in the gap for those around you. The end time revival will come as we prepare our hearts and stay focused, so we can pray. So to stay encouraged, we need to be prepared and lift one another up in prayer. By speaking the truth in love, we are able to minister to those who need the Lord, and bring them to a saving knowledge of Jesus.

Stay in Faith

As the world becomes more toxic, and many depart from the faith, we need to bring our lives under God's care and authority. We have to remain convinced that God will finish what He has started. The end time harvest will be dependent upon staying stirred up in our most holy faith and not losing heart as the times become harder. The harvest is reliant upon the people of God living according to God's way and not living as if He does not exist. As we stay in fellowship with the Lord, we will stand in the evil day and not lose heart. Challenging times may come, but as we stay in faith we are stable, not allowing every wind of doctrine to move us from our declaration of God's care and provision. We must keep the fire burning on the altar and stay filled with the Spirit, so we can bring Him glory, even in the fiery furnace of afflictions. David inquired of the Lord prior to battle and the Lord caused Him to triumph over his enemies, as he spoke the victory ahead of time and gave God the glory!

By allowing ourselves to be transformed by the renewing of our minds, we are able to resist the pressure of conforming to this world and it's dictates. This positions us to reap the benefits of holy living, as we come under God's authority and rule. We keep ourselves in a place of blessing as we yield to His ways and make them our ways. When we give God our best, we are able to see Him move on our behalf. God protects those who put Him first and those who worship Him with a pure and contrite heart. He is searching for a remnant who will worship Him in the beauty of His holiness. We bless others as we take what He has given us and pass it on. This brings prosperity and fruitfulness. We are bearing good fruit as we live to please Him. Worship gives us an opportunity to partake of heavenly realities, while still living in the earth realm. After all, we are seated with Him in heavenly places. We are highly favored and accepted in the beloved!

Just as the sons of Isaachar discerned the times and seasons, so we need discernment to understand all that will take place in the last days. The times ahead will be perilous, and we need to prepare for all that will take place. When we listen for God's voice, He will cause us to understand all that will transpire and give us direction.

The healing of the nations will bring forth an explosion of new converts that will usher in one of the biggest revivals the world has ever seen. But we must stay focused and allow the Lord to sift the wheat from the chaff and to prepare for the times ahead.

We are entering into a time of great travail, as the earth becomes shaken, we must keep our eyes on the Lord, so we can pray. We must be made ready as we become unveiled to the world. The Bride must avail herself to the Bridegroom (Jesus), to reap the benefits of holy living. In this way, we are able to partake of His majesty and glory in these end days.

In the story of Esther, Queen Vashti would not avail herself to the King, when he invited her to a feast. So King Ahasuerus sought out another bride who would rule with him and spend time in His chamber. As Esther became Queen, she spent time listening to the King, and gave Him her full attention. In this way, she gained favor to deliver the Jews from certain death, at the hand of Haman.

"Yet who knows whether you have come to the Kingdom for such a time as this?" (Esther 4:14). The ones who's hearts fail them not from fear, will be used to deliver those in gross darkness. They shall stand in the evil day and proclaim the good news of the Kingdom.

In conclusion, God is restoring the tabernacle of David in our midst. As we participate in God's pattern of worship, we become the carriers of His end time plan to restore, build up, and be a keeper of the anointing that will usher in the great harvest of souls. We must be diligent to protect this anointing and to allow God to take us to a place of restoring (our) tabernacle so we can partake of the mighty outpouring of His spirit in the days ahead. "So keep looking up for your redemption draws nigh," says the Lord.

BIBLIOGRAPHY

1. Rick Renner, *Sparkling Gems from the Greek, 365 Greek Word Studies for Every Day of the Year to Sharpen Your Understanding of God's Word*, Tulsa, Oklahoma. Teach All Nations, 2003.

2. David Swan, *The Power of Prophetic Worship*, Lumpur, Malaysia. Tan Suan (David Swan) 2001.

3. David Herzog, *Glory Invasion, Walking Under an Open Heaven*, Shippensburg, PA. Destiny Image Publishers. 2012.

4. Shane Warren Ministries, 2012. Shane Warren, *Secrets of the Well*. West Monroe, LA. Shane Warren Ministries, 2009.

5. Gabrielle Lichterman, *The Even Better Way to Beat Stress. Women's World*, Englewood Cliffs, New Jersey. April 15, 2013 issue.

6. New Spirit Filled Bible, New King James Version. Thomas Nelson, Publishing Inc. Co. 2002.

About the Author

Rhoda Banks is a Messianic Jew who came to the Lord at age twenty-four after responding to a series of prophetic dreams, where she saw Jesus on the cross who told her to believe in Him.

Shortly afterward, she attended Columbia University in New York and graduated with a master's in social work. While working in the field, she began to understand the importance of faith-based values. As a result, Rhoda attended Alliance Theology Seminary, before going into private practice in 1998.

She has a gift to teach and preach the word. She founded Recovery Ministries, a ministry designed to encourage, teach and heal the broken hearted in response to the Lord's call. Rhoda desires to see the body of Christ come into the wholeness for which Christ died. She is a respected pro- phetic voice, with an anointing for healing. Currently, she attends Bible School at Hope in Life Church in Carmel, New York.

Rhoda has been a Keynote Speaker at Women's Aglow Conferences, and other Seminars throughout the Northeast. She enjoys speaking on Worship, and has ministered on Worship teams throughout the years.

Rhoda has been in private practice for the past fifteen years. During this time, she has ministered to the lost and seen many lives transformed by the power of God. Her counseling background gives her a unique platform of instructing the Body of Christ, as well as inspiring them to walk in sound biblical principles.

She is a published author. She has written *Favor, The Overlooked Ingredient for Success*, and *The Purpose of Being Hidden*. This is her third published work.

Rhoda is available to speak at your church, Conference or Ministry meeting. Please contact her with details about your event.

Or to order her other resources, please contact her at:

Rhoda Banks, LCSW
246 Federal Rd. Suite C-33
Brookfield, Ct. 06804
email address: rhodabanks8@gmail.com
203-512-4914
203-775-6269

Prayer to receive Jesus as Lord and Savior

That if you confess with your mouth the Lord Jesus and believe in your heart that God raised him from the dead, you will be saved.

Rms. 10:9

Pray this prayer out loud:

Lord Jesus, I believe you died for me and I accept you into my heart as my Lord and Savior. I believe that you are the Son of God. I ask that you forgive my sins and cause me to walk in the new nature you have purchased for me. Change me into the person you have created me to be, even before the foundations of the world. I thank you that you have a perfect plan for me that is tailor made, and I decree that I will fulfill all that you have destined for me. Old things have passed away, all things have become new. I thank you for breathing new life into me and making me part of your family. I believe you not only died for me, but that you rose from the dead. So, I believe that I have eternal life in your name. I thank you Lord Jesus for saving me, and I am grateful and honored to accept your free gift of salvation that you poured out at Calvary. I give you all the praise and honor that's due your name.

Amen and Amen.

www.ingramcontent.com/pod-product-compliance
Lightning Source LLC
Chambersburg PA
CBHW060339130626
46553CB00003B/1059